Contents

❚ Words appearing in the text in bold, **like this**, are explained in the Glossary.

Heroin –
what's the deal?

Most people assume they'll never get caught in the heroin trap. But once someone starts taking heroin, their life can quickly spin out of control. This is what happened to Chris – and if you make the wrong decisions it could happen to you.

Chris first tried heroin when he was eighteen. He knew he had plenty of will power, so he didn't think it would hurt to try it once. He ended up in the bathroom vomiting, but he still found himself taking it again. Within a few weeks, he was thinking about heroin all the time – he had a serious problem.

Chris dropped out of college and lost touch with all his old friends. His life revolved around two things – taking heroin and getting the money to buy more. He didn't care what he did to get the money – shoplifting, burglary, even stealing from his family. Soon he was in trouble with the law and spent time in jail. He crashed two cars and **overdosed** twice, but somehow he survived – unlike many of his **addict** friends. When his girlfriend died from an overdose, he decided he had to stop the nightmare. He entered a **detox** clinic and after several attempts he finally got **clean**. Now Chris knows he's lucky to be alive.

"I can get up in the morning and remember what I did last night. I'm not in a panic to get my morning **fix**. I can go to the refrigerator (there's food in it now) and decide what I want to eat – yes, I actually have an appetite! And I don't have any dates in court. At last I'm free to live my life."

A deadly habit

Taking heroin is one of the riskiest things anyone can ever do. It can completely take over a person's life, ruin their health, and drive them to take up crime. Heroin addicts often die young – either from an overdose or from infections. So why do people ever start?

Making decisions

You might think that heroin will never be an issue for you. But if you were tempted to try it, or even became addicted, what would you do? This book aims to give you the information you need to help you make your own decisions about heroin. It looks at what heroin does to a user's health and explains why the drug is so addictive. There are also many issues to think about. What's the right way to tackle the heroin problem? How can addicts be helped to kick their deadly habit?

Get ready to take a long, hard look at heroin.

■ Once someone has started taking heroin, it's very easy for their life to enter a downward spiral.

5

Heroin is a form of **opium** – a very powerful drug with a long history of **abuse**. For thousands of years, people have used opium to relieve pain, but also to escape from reality. There have always been opium **addicts** – people whose lives have been ruined by **dependence** on the drug.

❚ Heroin is produced from the fluid found inside the seed heads of the opium poppy.

Like other forms of opium, heroin comes from the opium poppy, which is mainly grown in South East Asia, especially in Burma, Laos, and Thailand. Other major growing areas for opium poppies are Afghanistan, Pakistan, Colombia, and Mexico.

What's in opium?

The two main ingredients in opium are **morphine** and **codeine**. Both of these substances are processed into a range of medical drugs, which are used as painkillers. Morphine has the effect of changing people's moods, dulling their senses, and cutting them off from the world, while making them feel sleepy and relaxed.

A history of abuse

Ever since opium was first discovered, people growing and harvesting opium poppies have also smoked the drug to make their lives seem easier. Many of these opium farmers became addicted to the drug. But they were not the only ones to become **hooked** on opium.

By the eighteenth century, China was famous for its **opium dens**, where people lay or sat on couches smoking opium in clay pipes.

In the nineteenth century, laudanum – a mixture of alcohol and opium – was developed as a painkiller. However, it was widely abused in Europe and the United States, and many people became laudanum addicts.

! Sleep bringers

The Latin name of the opium poppy is *Papaver somniferum*, which means "sleep bringer". All **opiates** – substances made from the opium poppy – produce a feeling of drowsiness and relaxation.

The birth of heroin

In 1898, the Bayer drug company created a new medical drug from morphine. This new drug was very fast acting and more than twice as strong as morphine. Its medical name was **diamorphine**, although it soon became known as heroin. Diamorphine began to be widely used for emergency pain relief. However, by the 1920s, some people had begun to inject themselves with the drug. Heroin became available for sale on the streets and the deadly habit of heroin abuse had begun.

▌Chinese addicts in an opium den, in the early twentieth century. Some opium smokers were so strongly addicted that they spent most of their lives in these dens.

The heroin sold by **dealers** on the streets usually takes the form of a white or brownish powder. This powder can be "**snorted**" (sniffed) or smoked. It can also be dissolved in water and injected. Because street heroin is produced and sold illegally, there are no controls over the powder's strength or what it is mixed with. People may die either from taking too much heroin (because the mixture is too pure) or from the dangerous substances mixed with the heroin.

A deadly cut

Heroin sold by dealers on the streets is mixed or "**cut**" with a range of less expensive substances to increase the dealers' profits. Often heroin dealers aren't too fussy about what they use. Many of these substances are dangerous in themselves and when they are mixed with heroin they create a truly lethal mixture.

Heroin is sometimes mixed with powdered milk, sugar, baking soda, or talcum powder – and these are some of the safer substances! It is sometimes also cut with laundry detergent, gravel, and even strychnine (a poison used to kill rats). All of these additives are extremely dangerous when they are injected into a user's veins, or **inhaled** into their lungs.

Different strengths

Because street heroin is mixed with other substances, it is impossible to know just how pure the drug really is. Heroin purity can vary from 10 to 90 per cent, although most street heroin is around 60 per cent pure. With no way of telling the strength and purity of the drug they are taking, heroin users just have to guess. This means it is easy for them to get it wrong and take too much – an **overdose**. This is how many heroin overdoses occur.

Black tar heroin

Heroin usually takes the form of powder, but recently a black, gummy form of heroin has appeared in the United States. Called Mexican Black or black tar heroin, it is made in Mexico using crude processing methods. Black tar heroin is impure and very dangerous if injected. Some users who have injected it into their veins have developed botulism – a form of severe poisoning that affects the **central nervous system** and often results in death.

! Street names for heroin

Street names for heroin include: junk, smack, H, mojo, brown, skag, and China White. Whatever name it's given, it's still a killer.

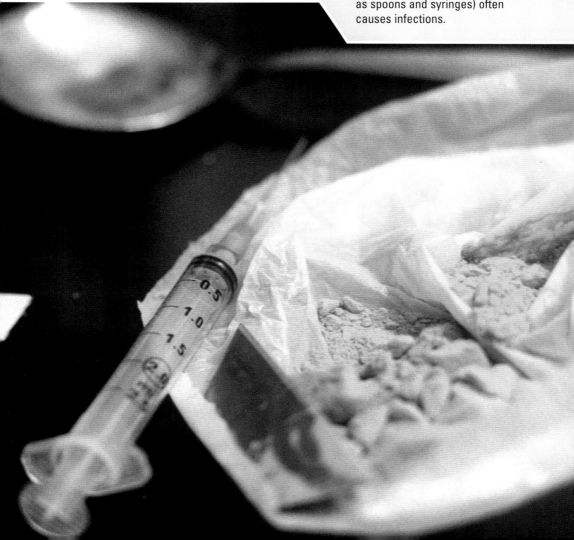

▌ Heroin is usually sold as a brown or white powder, which is diluted and injected with a syringe. The equipment that addicts use (such as spoons and syringes) often causes infections.

Most heroin **addicts** inject themselves with a solution of heroin powder, but the drug can be taken in other ways as well. Recently, there has been a marked increase in **chasing** and **snorting** heroin. These methods are especially popular among young heroin users, who see them as safer than injecting. But many of these young users don't realize they are still putting their lives at risk.

Shooting up

Injecting heroin into the body using a syringe is often known as "shooting up". It is the method used by most addicts, as it delivers large amounts of the drug rapidly into the bloodstream. Injection is usually **intravenous** – directly into a vein – and the drug takes effect within ten seconds. Some users inject heroin into a muscle or under the skin – methods that produce effects in five to eight minutes. Some addicts inject themselves up to four times in one day.

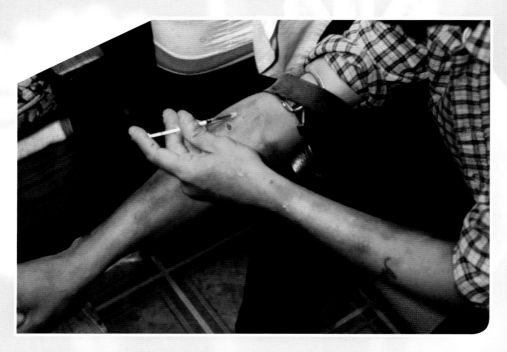

▌Many heroin addicts inject the drug directly into their veins. Over a period of time this leads to damaged veins and serious **circulation** problems.

I Users often use a candle to heat up heroin powder on tinfoil. This method of taking heroin is sometimes seen as relatively harmless – but it may still result in death.

Chasing the dragon

Another method of taking heroin was invented in Hong Kong in the 1950s. Known as "chasing the dragon", it involves heating powdered heroin on a piece of tinfoil and then breathing in the fumes that are given off. This method became popular in Europe in the late 1980s. It attracted a different type of user – people who did not want to inject themselves. This had the result of making heroin use much more widespread.

Snorting heroin

While chasing the dragon became popular in Europe, a different kind of heroin use was developing in the United States. Here, users often snort or sniff heroin powder up through their nose, using a "quill" of rolled-up paper. Snorting carries many health risks as it damages the nasal passages, throat, and lungs.

Safer alternatives?

Some people believe that snorting and chasing heroin are not very risky. They claim that because these methods avoid the risks directly linked to injecting, they are relatively harmless. But this is simply not true.

Whatever the method used, heroin-taking involves many health risks (see pages 24–29). It is also very addictive. Most people who start by simply giving heroin a try will become addicts – and most of these will end up injecting the drug.

! Teenagers at risk

- According to a recent US survey, 87 per cent of smokers and snorters of heroin are under the age of 26.

- In another survey of US high-school students, 40 per cent of those questioned said that they didn't believe there was a great risk in trying heroin – so long as they didn't inject.

What sort of people take heroin? The answer is all sorts. Nowadays, there is a growing trend for people with well-paid jobs to turn to heroin, and there are far more female **addicts** than in the past. Heroin **dealers** are also targeting younger people. However, the good news is that heroin use amongst teenagers appears to be stable, or even falling.

 Sometimes, heroin use starts very young – a few people experiment with heroin even before they are in their teens.

Question

Are large numbers of teenagers trying heroin?

Changing patterns

There was a time when most heroin takers were either super-rich rock stars or down-and-out "**junkies**". But patterns of heroin use have changed as the drug has become more widely available. Nowadays, heroin can be bought in small towns as well as inner cities. It is packaged in smaller quantities than before, making it seem less expensive. The practices of **snorting** and **chasing** have made it seem more acceptable to groups of people who would previously have steered clear of heroin.

Teenage trends

Recent figures show that some young people are trying heroin in their early teens, with a significant number starting as young as twelve years old. These trends are extremely worrying because evidence shows that those who start a drug habit young will experience the greatest difficulty in kicking their habit later.

A new kind of user

Over the last ten years, heroin use has risen dramatically amongst the relatively well-off. Many men and women with successful careers have taken up the habit of snorting or chasing heroin. These new kinds of user insist they are not addicts and believe that they are safe from many of the problems that heroin brings. However, they are taking enormous risks. They may still die from an **overdose** and suffer all the bad effects of impure heroin. They also run the daily risk of losing their job and everything they've worked for if their illegal habit is discovered.

❗ Teenage heroin use

- In the United Kingdom, between 5 and 10 per cent of 15-year-olds have been offered heroin.

- In the United States, heroin use by 12th graders (aged around 17) increased by more than 100 per cent from 1990 to 2000. However, the number of heroin users in this age group has fallen in the last few years.

Answer

No. Only a tiny minority of teenagers try heroin. Those who do try it are putting their lives at risk.

Nobody can avoid the stark fact that heroin is a killer drug. Yet, despite all the harm it can do, people still take it. So what are the pressures that drive some people to take up the drug?

"I was at this party when lots of people started snorting heroin. A girl I really like came up to me and told me it was great – she said I should join in too. I have to admit I was tempted, but then I decided I just wasn't happy with it. Now I'm really pleased I said no. The next time I saw the girl, she looked terrible. She told me she was trying to get off the stuff, but it was really hard. She also said I should never start."

Kevin, a teenager who decided to say no

A deadly adventure

For many young heroin users, their first experience of trying the drug is driven by the desire to take risks and be daring. They may see taking heroin as an act of defiance or a way to rebel against their parents. But what kind of gesture of freedom is it, if they end up throwing all their chances away?

The great escape?

Other people may try heroin because they think that it will help them escape from their problems. They may have heard about the feelings the drug can give and be tempted to try it – especially if their life is not going well. Studies have shown that the young people most likely to use heroin are also experiencing major life problems. Many young heroin users also have to deal with very poor housing, unemployment, and violence in the home.

Dealer pressure

Sometimes, a heroin habit starts when someone who is already using "soft drugs", such as cannabis, is persuaded by **dealers** or other drug users to try "something different".

Some drug dealers work very hard to sell hard drugs, such as heroin, to young people. They know that once someone has tried heroin, there is a very good chance that they will become **addicted**. This will provide the dealers with a regular source of income.

Joining in?

Some young people may feel under pressure from their friends or other people they know. They may be at a party or in a group where some of their friends are **chasing** or **snorting** heroin. Or they may be persuaded by someone who has tried the drug.

At times like these it's very important to remember that nobody has the right to make your decisions for you. This is especially true when the decision you make could mean putting your life in danger.

▌Some young people may feel under pressure to experiment with drugs. But the vast majority of teenagers never try heroin.

Is heroin cool? Sometimes images in the **media** seem to say so. The fact that it's a killer may even be seen to add to its dangerous, glamorous image. But is a habit that takes away your looks, your chances to have fun – and even your life – really so cool? Should the music and fashion industries be sending out messages that it's OK to take heroin?

Inspiration or thief?

Many talented people have become caught in the heroin trap. Musicians, artists, writers, and actors have believed that it would help their art. Some of them have spent years struggling with their **addiction**. Others have died because of it.

The list of celebrities whose addiction helped to lead to their early death includes the rock musicians Kurt Cobain, Layne Staley, and Shannon Hoon, the comedian John Belushi, the actor River Phoenix, and the artist Jean-Michel Basquiat. All of them died young – killed by heroin. Just think what all these people might have gone on to produce if they hadn't got **hooked** on heroin.

▌ Layne Staley was the lead singer and songwriter with the Seattle-based band Alice in Chains. He is just one of many artists and musicians whose lives have been cut short by heroin.

Heroin chic?

It's hard to imagine that anyone could ever see heroin addicts as glamorous – but that's exactly how New York photographer Davide Sorrenti tried to present them. In the 1990s, Sorrenti took fashion shots of his **junkie** friends and started a trend for "heroin chic". The fashion took off and many advertisements featured thin, wasted-looking people. In 1997 Sorrenti died from a drug **overdose** and his images of junkies were revealed as tragic rather than cool. But who knows how many young people were helped along the road to heroin by those photos?

❚ In the late 1990s, fashion photos like this promoted the idea of "heroin chic", suggesting that it was cool to look super-thin and wasted.

Viewpoints

The music and fashion industries have a very strong influence on young people, but should they be responsible for sending out the "right" messages about drugs?

- **The music and fashion industries need to act responsibly about drugs**
  Young people are easily influenced by music and fashion. This means that musicians and fashion photographers are in a position of great power. They need to think very carefully before they send out dangerous messages about drugs to the public. These powerful people should act responsibly and not put young lives at risk.

- **Drug awareness and health care are not the responsibility of the music and fashion industries**
  Musicians and fashion photographers are artists and they should be free to express themselves however they want. It's the job of other organizations to issue warnings about drugs – and the public should be free to make up their own minds.

What do you think?

What does heroin do?

Heroin has a powerful impact on the minds and bodies of its users. The drug's first dramatic effects take place very soon after it enters the body. For many people, their first experience of heroin is extremely scary, as they feel themselves losing control of their bodies.

Question

How long do the effects of heroin usually last?

A sudden rush

After injecting heroin, most users report feeling a sudden surge of warmth and relaxation – rather like the "high" that people experience after they have done a lot of exercise. This initial sensation is often known as a "rush" and it lasts for only a few minutes. It is accompanied by

▌ After a shot of heroin, users feel cut off from their surroundings, as if in a trance. They may also feel scared, dizzy, and sick.

a range of less enjoyable symptoms and feelings, including a dry mouth and a sense of heaviness in the limbs. Many users also experience **nausea**, dizziness, and vomiting at this stage. Others have intensely itchy skin and feel very restless.

Going on the nod

Following the initial rush, heroin users enter a drowsy, trance-like state. This is sometimes known as "going on the nod". In this state, which may last up to six hours, the user's pulse and breathing slow down dramatically. The **central nervous system** ceases to function properly and the brain fails to respond to many of the body's usual signals.

Breathing problems

As heroin users enter the trance-like state they start breathing much more shallowly. Sometimes, the breathing reflexes close down completely, causing the user to suffocate and die.

Other dangers

While people are "on the nod" their thinking becomes very vague. They are not properly aware of things going on around them or of how much time has passed. They also feel no pain, cold, hunger, stress, anxiety, or fear. This state can be very dangerous, as people fail to react to risks around them. If they fail to keep themselves warm, they may suffer from hypothermia (a very serious condition in which the body temperature becomes dangerously low).

Answer

Around four to six hours. For almost all of this time, the user is in a trance-like state, sometimes known as being "on the nod".

"I've had one go at **chasing the dragon** and that was enough. I felt really weird – hot, itchy, and dizzy. After that I was so spaced out I didn't know what I was doing. I kept dozing off and then waking up with a start, feeling in a panic. I don't ever want to feel like that again."

Kelly, aged eighteen

How does heroin affect the body and the brain? What is it about the drug that makes it so **addictive**? Health professionals, chemists, and other scientists have run studies on groups of heroin addicts and have come up with some very worrying findings.

Question

What is physical addiction?

❙ The musician Kurt Cobain, lead singer with the US rock band Nirvana, struggled for years with his addiction to heroin. When he died suddenly at the age of 27 (he is thought to have committed suicide), experts found enough heroin in his body to have killed three addicts.

What happens in the brain?

Like all forms of **opium**, heroin contains chemicals known as **opiates**. When someone takes heroin, these opiates enter their bloodstream and travel to the brain. In the brain, the opiates stimulate special **receptors** that spread a feeling of warmth and pleasure throughout the body. The receptors also suppress the body's **central nervous system**, preventing the user from experiencing pain.

Wanting more

Once someone has experienced the "high" produced by heroin, their body **craves** that experience again – even though the person's reason tells them to keep well away. Heroin is such a powerful drug that it's usual to feel cravings even after a single dose. Most people find it very hard to resist this strong physical urge, and give in to their cravings.

One of the great dangers of heroin is that it seems to offer a solution to life's problems. People look back at the time when they were in a heroin trance – experiencing no worry or pain – and long to feel like that again. But if they give in to heroin, their problems will really begin.

Heroin addiction

Once someone starts taking heroin regularly, their brain and body begin to rely on its effects. Within a very short time they may become physically addicted to or **dependent** on the drug just in order to function. When someone is physically addicted to a drug, they suffer a range of very unpleasant symptoms if they stop taking it (see page 23). Addicts may start feeling these **withdrawal symptoms** less than a day after they last took heroin.

❚ Once someone is **hooked** on heroin, they will do anything to get more of their drug. Most **dealers** are only too happy to see addicts coming back for more.

Answer

Physical addiction or dependence is when a person's body becomes so used to the presence of a drug that they need to keep using it in order to feel well. When the person stops using the drug, they become ill with unpleasant withdrawal symptoms.

How long do withdrawal symptoms last?

More and more

At the same time as a heroin **addict** is becoming physically addicted to the drug, their brain is also developing a **tolerance** to its effects. This means that addicts need larger and larger doses of heroin to achieve the same effects that they experienced when they first tried the drug.

The dual effects of addiction and tolerance mean that heroin users get locked into a vicious circle. In a very short space of time, they start to take larger and larger doses. They also take the drug at more and more frequent intervals. The final result is often death from an **overdose**.

Desperate cravings

It's a very big mistake to think that heroin addicts spend their time experiencing "highs". In fact, the opposite is true. Most addicts don't take heroin to feel good. The harsh truth is they need to keep taking the drug to stop them feeling bad. In fact, most of the time heroin addicts feel very bad indeed.

"It was the worst thing I've ever been through. Every part of my body ached – even my teeth. I was sick. I had the runs. I kept burning up and then feeling freezing cold. And all the time I was thinking, 'I could stop this any time, if I just took another shot.'"

Kim, an ex-heroin addict, describing the experience of withdrawing from heroin

Within four to six hours of their last **fix**, regular heroin users begin to feel desperate for more. Addicts describe feeling very low and depressed and experiencing an overwhelming longing for the temporary comfort that a dose of heroin can provide. They also describe the sensation of their whole body crying out for more, as it **craves** the feelings that heroin delivers. At this stage, most users give in to their cravings. But even if they manage to resist, there are harder tests to come.

Withdrawal symptoms

About eight to twelve hours after their last dose of heroin, addicts begin to experience physical symptoms. The first signs of withdrawal from heroin are usually watering eyes and an aching sensation. This is just the start of a series of **withdrawal symptoms** that include:

■ restlessness and an inability to sleep

■ aching bones and muscles

■ frequent vomiting and diarrhoea

■ excessive sweating

■ stomach pains

■ sudden chills and shivering fits.

Once someone is suffering in this way, it's only natural for them to want to take the drug again. People need enormous will power to resist the urge to take another dose of heroin when they know that it will make them feel better again, even if only temporarily.

Answer

Withdrawal symptoms usually last around a week to ten days.

▌The horrors of withdrawal from heroin include aching bones, sweating, vomiting, and diarrhoea.

Sooner or later, most heroin **addicts** have a really bad experience. This might be an **overdose**, or another problem caused by the way their body reacts to the drug. If they are lucky, they will simply end up being very ill, but for many it means death. Overdoses don't just happen to addicts – they may occur the very first time a person tries heroin.

Poison in the veins

Street heroin comes mixed with a range of dangerous substances (see page 8) and some of these may cause serious harm or even death. Deaths have been reported from injections of heroin mixed with strychnine (a poison used to kill rats). Other substances mixed with the heroin may cause sudden blood clots or heart attacks.

Mixing drugs

A frequent cause of death among heroin addicts is the very risky practice of combining drugs. One particularly lethal combination is the "speedball" – a mixture of heroin and crack cocaine, which is often

"We'd gone to this open-air concert. I was having a good time but then I realized I hadn't seen Kate for ages. I searched around for a bit, but then I found her all on her own lying behind a tent. She was lying really still and her face had gone blue. I didn't know what to do – I was so scared. In the end we got an ambulance but it was too late. They said she'd had a heroin overdose – they could still see the powder all up her nose. I just couldn't believe it. I know for a fact she'd never tried heroin before."

Gemma, a teenager, describing what happened to her friend the first time she tried heroin

Question

Is there anything you can do to help someone who has taken an overdose of heroin?

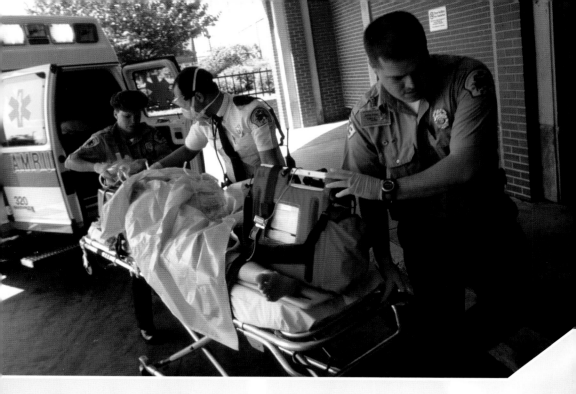

■ Heroin overdose often ends in death. However, there is an antidote, so if a medical team manages to reach the victim in time, they may be able to save their life.

cited as a cause of death. It is also very risky to mix heroin with alcohol.

Overdosing

Overdosing is frighteningly common among heroin takers. Because there is no way of knowing the strength of a dose of heroin, it is very easy for addicts to inject themselves with too much of the drug. This may happen the first time someone uses the drug.

Sometimes death by overdose may happen quickly – as the heart immediately stops beating. Some people have died before they have even had time to pull the needle out of their vein. At other times, an overdose happens as the drug slowly closes the breathing system down and the victim suffocates and dies.

Answer

Yes. Lie the person on their side so that they do not choke. Then phone the emergency services straightaway. Ask for an ambulance and explain that the person has taken heroin. There is an **antidote** to heroin – called naloxone – which can quickly reverse the drug's effects on the body.

Heroin **addicts** plunge needles into their bodies several times a day. Health problems caused by needles and other equipment range from painful abscesses (a kind of large boil) to death from AIDS, **hepatitis**, or blood poisoning.

Dirty needles

Using dirty needles leads to a range of skin infections, including open, weeping sores and abscesses. Dirty needles can also have the result of poisoning a user's blood. Addicts suffering from blood poisoning sometimes need to have a limb amputated and some may even die.

HIV and hepatitis

If an addict shares a needle with another addict, their blood will mingle. This means that if either person has an infection, it may be passed on to the other. Some of the infections transmitted by shared needles are major killers, such as **HIV** (which causes AIDS) and hepatitis.

Needle exchange

In the 1980s, some governments realized that they were facing an **epidemic** of HIV/AIDS and hepatitis amongst drug users. This was not simply a problem for the addicts. Drug users were

❙ Needle exchange programmes for heroin users have dramatically reduced the number of new HIV infections among addicts. But not everyone is in favour of the programmes.

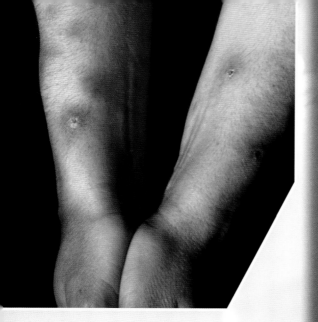

▌ People who inject heroin often have dark scars on their arms, sometimes called tracks.

also giving birth to babies with HIV and passing their infections on to their partners. Some action was needed to stop the spread of infections amongst heroin users – but what could be done?

In many countries, governments have authorized the setting up of needle exchange programmes. These programmes involve collecting used needles and replacing them with **sterile** new ones. There is evidence that needle exchange programmes have made a real difference. An evaluation of a programme in New Haven, United States, revealed that it had reduced the rate of new HIV infection in the area by around 33 per cent. The programme also helped more than 1,000 people to enter treatment for drug addiction.

Viewpoints

Needle exchange programmes have been shown to have positive results, but not everyone is in favour of them.

● **Needle exchange programmes are a good thing**

It is very hard to educate drug users about the risks of contracting dangerous diseases, so needle exchange programmes provide a practical way of preventing the spread of infections such as HIV. The programmes protect the addicts and also help to safeguard the rest of the population.

● **Needle exchange programmes send the wrong message to people**

Handing out needles to drug addicts is a way of helping them to keep using heroin. This gives the wrong message, as it suggests that society approves of their habit. Taking heroin is against the law and it is wrong for people to appear to be encouraging drug use.

What do you think?

Long-term effects

Many heroin **addicts** die young, but for those who manage to survive, there are a host of long-term problems to be faced. Not only do addicts have to live with many painful and even life-threatening physical effects, but their mental health is also affected.

Serious health effects

People who have been injecting heroin for several years usually suffer from long-term damage to their **circulation** system. Many of the substances mixed with the heroin do not dissolve easily in the blood and so clog up the blood vessels and other organs. In the long-term, this results in serious damage to the veins and to the lining and valves of the heart. Heroin addicts are also at increased risk from strokes (in which the flow of blood to the brain is suddenly interrupted).

Other serious physical problems caused by taking heroin include damage to the liver, kidneys, and brain. Addicts are also likely to suffer from lung infections and respiratory diseases, especially **tuberculosis** and **pneumonia**.

Some heroin addicts experience problems in their joints, developing arthritis and rheumatism. Because heroin users tend to neglect their health, and eat unhealthily, many suffer from **malnutrition**. Long-term heroin users may also have problems with their digestive system, and low resistance to **viruses** and other illnesses.

Mental health problems

As well as all the harmful physical effects of taking heroin, there are also **psychological** ones, as the heroin habit affects a user's feelings and moods. Addicts usually feel lonely and cut off from their family and friends. Addicts worry all the time about how to get their next **fix** – and how to find the money for it. There is also the constant fear that they will get into serious trouble with the law.

Most heroin addicts also have to face the fact that their habit has forced them to sacrifice lots of things they value. For many people, taking heroin means saying goodbye to a good career or a comfortable home. Many addicts lose everything and are forced to live rough, sinking into a life of crime to feed their habit. But even for those addicts who can afford to buy the drug, there are still the constant fears of **overdosing**, and all the worries about the threats to their health. Taken altogether, it's not at all surprising that most heroin users are very seriously depressed.

▌Many heroin addicts who live on the streets suffer from depression, as they see their hopes of a healthy, happy life disappearing.

Broken lives

Taking heroin changes people's lives in many ways – and none of them for the better. Heroin users often drop out of normal, everyday life. Some **addicts** are also forced to turn to crime, simply to find the money to fund their habit.

❚ Heroin addicts often end up on the streets, begging for money in order to survive.

Family and friends

Once people start taking heroin regularly, they find that the drug begins to take over their lives. Often the first things to go are family and friends. New heroin addicts often find that they are spending more and more time with their heroin-taking friends, and quickly lose touch with their old life.

Many young heroin addicts move out of home as family tensions caused by their habit become too hard to handle. Sometimes a specific incident – such as an addict stealing from a parent's purse – becomes the sparking point for a family row. As a result, the addict may decide that it's no longer possible to continue living at home.

Once a young addict has left home, more problems begin. It's very hard for addicts to find places to stay. As a result, many young addicts find themselves living rough, staying illegally in empty buildings, or even sleeping on the streets.

Losing jobs

Most heroin addicts find it almost impossible to hold down a job. They spend large amounts of their time either being "spaced out" when they are taking heroin, or feeling terrible when they are **craving** the drug. This doesn't leave much time to concentrate on work. Without regular money to pay rent, they may quickly find themselves on the streets.

Turning to crime

Heroin is expensive and very few addicts have enough money to fund their habit. This leaves only one option – crime. Heroin addicts turn to a range of illegal activities to get money. They may steal money from their family and friends or commit burglaries. Many of them also start shoplifting. This may involve taking items that they can sell in exchange for money. It may also mean stealing the things they need, such as food.

A large number of addicts, but especially girls, get involved in **prostitution**, earning money in return for sex. To many of them, this seems at first a quick and easy way to earn money. But they soon discover that it is very risky. Prostitutes are at risk both from sexually transmitted infections (STIs) and from violence.

▌Most heroin addicts need to find at least £500 a week to support their habit, so many of them end up breaking the law.

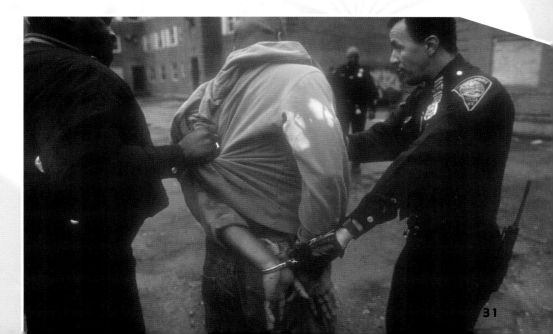

Babies and children at risk

Taking heroin doesn't just affect the lives of **addicts**. It also causes problems and distress to many others – including families, friends, and partners. But the ones who suffer most of all are the addicts' children. Before they are even born, the babies of heroin addicts are put at risk in many ways.

Heroin and pregnancy

When heroin addicts become pregnant, they suffer from a range of serious problems that affect their own health and the health of their unborn children. Nearly half of heroin-addicted women suffer from problems during pregnancy, such as **anaemia**, heart disease, **pneumonia**, or **hepatitis**. These conditions seriously weaken the mother, making her more likely to have a **miscarriage**. Heroin addicts often give birth to still-born infants (babies who are dead at birth) or babies who are premature (born before they have fully developed in the womb).

Denise's story

For some heroin addicts, the news that they are pregnant marks a turning point in their lives. This is what happened to Denise.

*"I'd been taking heroin for about five years before I got pregnant. I never thought about the future – just survived. But when this happened to me I knew I had to stop. I'd seen my friend's baby die and it was terrible. So I went **cold turkey** – the day after I got the [pregnancy test] result. It was hell, but I got through it. Now I'm living back at home. I can't say it's easy, but the baby's lovely. I'm really pleased I did it because of him."*

■ The babies of heroin addicts need round-the-clock care in order to survive their first few weeks of life.

Infant addicts

Babies born to heroin addicts can suffer from a range of health problems. Most babies of heroin addicts are seriously underweight when they are born. They may have difficulties with their heart and lungs, and they may suffer from mental development problems. Many of these serious health problems will stay with the children all their lives.

All these problems are bad enough, but most distressing of all is the fact that these babies are born addicted to heroin. After months of receiving a regular supply of the drug through their mother's blood, their tiny bodies have become addicted to it.

Heroin addiction in newborn babies is an extremely dangerous condition and needs very careful treatment. The infant needs to be weaned off the drug as soon as possible, but this involves going through painful **withdrawal symptoms**. This is hard enough for an adult, but it is much harder for a tiny infant, and heroin-addicted babies often die within a few days or weeks of birth.

Children at risk

The risks don't stop at babyhood for the children of heroin **addicts**. These vulnerable children, who may already be unwell, face a terrifying range of hazards as they grow up with heroin as a part of their everyday life.

Neglect and danger

Most children of heroin addicts do not have a stable home. During their childhood, most of them will move home many times, and they may have several different carers. Children of addicts often live in poverty and have a chaotic lifestyle, with irregular meals and bedtimes.

Because their parents and carers are under the influence of heroin much of the time, these children often suffer accidents, and serious illnesses may go untreated. They may even suffer from **malnutrition** because of an unhealthy diet.

All these problems are worrying enough, but there are also specific dangers that come from living with people who are injecting drugs. Children of addicts may have horrible accidents caused by abandoned needles (which may be infected). They may accidentally swallow heroin that has been left lying around. They are also confronted with the daily reality of seeing people injecting heroin. Before they reach adulthood, these children stand the chance of losing a parent or carer to an **overdose** and they will also almost certainly witness violence. All of these factors contribute to the likelihood that the children will also develop a drugs habit.

Helping the children

In most **developed countries**, serious attempts are made to help the children of heroin addicts. Social workers visit problem homes, and teachers and youth workers keep a lookout for children who are showing signs of distress and neglect. Children who are in real danger are taken into care, while others are monitored carefully. There are also several organizations that children in trouble may contact if they need help and support. You can find out more about these organizations on pages 54–55 of this book.

▮ Children who grow up in poverty often develop health problems and need special care from social workers.

⚠ Children of addicts

The number of children living with addicts is very large. In the United Kingdom, for example, there is one child for every problem drug user.

For many heroin **addicts**, there comes a point where they decide they have to give up the drug. Kicking the habit isn't at all easy, but there are plenty of organizations whose job is to help addicts break free from heroin.

Question

What does it mean to "go cold turkey"?

▌Giving up heroin is very hard, but it is possible to recover from heroin addiction and live a happier, healthier life again.

Deciding to stop

There are a vast number of reasons why people decide to stop taking heroin. They may have had a frightening experience while they were on heroin. They may also be concerned about their health, worried about being arrested, and depressed about the fact that their lives are going nowhere.

Sometimes, the terrible shock of seeing a friend die from an **overdose** may make an addict decide to kick their habit. But there are positive reasons too. In some cases, a new relationship may persuade an addict to decide to make changes in their life. For some young women, the discovery that they are pregnant may help them to make the decision to give up – for the sake of their unborn child as well as themself (see Denise's story on page 32).

Different approaches

Experts have identified three main approaches to giving up heroin – and most of them agree that it's best when all three of these are combined. The three approaches are:

- **detoxification** (or detox) – the process of withdrawing heroin from the body. For most heroin addicts, this is a difficult and painful process.

- **substitution** – treating someone by substituting a prescribed dose of a less harmful drug, such as **methadone**, in the place of heroin. This allows the addict's body to adjust to life without heroin.

- **therapy** – the process of talking through difficulties with an expert helper. Therapy helps people to learn ways to deal with their **cravings** and to resist the temptation to take the drug again.

Detoxification

Detoxification literally means "removing poison". This is what happens when a regular heroin user stops taking the drug. However, because a heroin addict's body has become used to the drug's effects, it usually reacts dramatically. Within twelve hours, the user experiences the range of painful **withdrawal symptoms** described on page 23.

Answer

When someone says they are "going cold turkey" they mean they are giving up heroin suddenly and completely, and not substituting anything else in its place. The name comes from the goosebumps that appear on the skin when someone withdraws from heroin (or another drug). These goosebumps, which make the skin look like that of a plucked turkey, are combined with chills and shivers.

▌Detoxification leaves the heroin user feeling sick, sweaty, and achy.

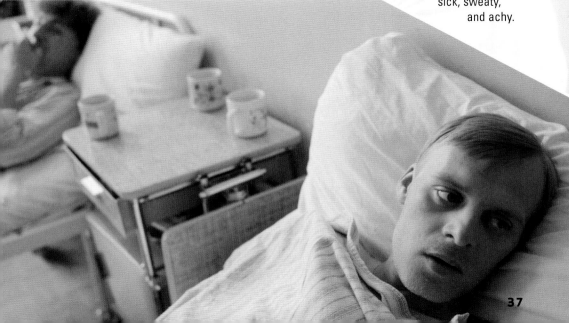

Powerful cravings

While a small proportion of heroin **addicts** manage to give up the drug simply by going "**cold turkey**", most heroin users find this method of quitting incredibly hard. Their bodies still **crave** heroin long after they have given it up, and some still feel these cravings several years after giving up the drug. Fortunately, there are methods to help people to overcome their cravings and turn their backs on heroin for good.

Substitution

Methadone is the main drug that is used as a substitute for heroin. It allows addicts to adjust gradually to life without heroin, while not suffering unpleasant **withdrawal symptoms**. Methadone acts on the brain in a similar way to an **opiate**, so it removes the cravings that heroin addicts experience. But it does not make people "high", and when it is properly **prescribed** by a doctor, methadone does not make people sleepy or "spaced out". However, people can become addicted to methadone and may find it very hard to stop using the drug. Methadone doses must be carefully monitored, to make sure that people do not exceed the recommended doses.

▌ Every day, around 115,000 Americans take methadone. Recent US studies have found that two thirds of methadone patients show a dramatic decrease in heroin use, and a greatly reduced involvement in crime.

Therapy

Most experts agree that heroin users who are trying to quit their habit can be greatly helped by behavioural **therapy**. This involves trying to find ways to change a person's behaviour so that they can deal better with their problems.

Behavioural therapy may be conducted in one-to-one sessions or in groups. Some programmes try to help people find new ways to cope with their problems, rather than turning to drugs. In other programmes, recovering addicts can win vouchers as a reward for staying **clean**, and these vouchers can be exchanged for items that encourage healthy living.

Viewpoints

Methadone has been proved to be an effective method of helping addicts give up heroin. However, methadone programmes are expensive and not everyone thinks they are a good idea.

- **Methadone helps heroin addicts and society**

When people with a heroin problem are given the drug methadone instead, they find it easier to stop using heroin and have the chance to live a useful life. If they were denied their regular dose of methadone, many of these people would become heroin addicts once again, and cause many problems for themselves and society.

- **Prescribing methadone is not the answer**

Prescribing methadone to heroin addicts simply substitutes one addictive drug for another. It does not make people free from drugs or free from addiction. Society should not be expected to pay to look after ex-heroin addicts, simply because they cannot live without drugs.

What do you think?

The heroin business

Heroin is very big business. While **addicts** are dying penniless on the streets, the **drug barons** who run the heroin business are pocketing enormous fortunes. They operate behind the scenes, controlling every stage of the heroin business – from the growing of **opium** to the sale of heroin on the streets – and at every stage they profit from the misery and desperation of others.

Secret power

The illegal drugs business has been compared to the worldwide car industry, both in its scale and in the size of its profits – which means that the drug barons wield incredible power. They control a vast network of smugglers and **dealers**. Through this network, heroin reaches streets all over the world. However, it is very rare for the big players to be caught. It is the dealers on the street (who are usually heroin addicts themselves) or the people who are persuaded to carry drugs over borders, who end up getting arrested and sent to prison.

❚ Heroin is often smuggled across borders, concealed in secret compartments in trucks or other vehicles.

Taking control

The drug barons who control the heroin trade work on an international scale. They play a major part in the economy of the countries where the opium poppy is grown, and keep most of the income earned by the poor opium farmers. Opium is grown in some of the poorest regions of the world and yet one of these areas is known as the "golden triangle", because it provides such enormous profits for the drug barons.

As well as making sure that most of the money from the sale of heroin finds its way into their pockets, the international drug barons also exert a huge amount of control over the politics of opium-growing countries. Because they are so powerful, they can even decide where wars will be fought. Many **terrorist** organizations worldwide are funded by money made from heroin.

▌While the opium farmers barely scratch a living, the drug barons who control the heroin trade are pocketing vast fortunes.

❗ Drugs trade facts

- The illegal drugs trade represents over 8 per cent of all international trade.

- It has been estimated that the illegal drugs trade is worth US$400 thousand million (£210 thousand million) a year – that's more than the worldwide trade in motor vehicles.

Dirty dealing

In order to get heroin to the users, the people who control the drugs industry pull some very dirty tricks. Smuggling heroin across country borders involves enormous risks for the people who carry the drugs. The business of drug dealing is also corrupt. A vast network of **dealers** is controlled by a few very rich people who own the central supplies of the drug.

Smuggling heroin

The **drug barons** find many ways to smuggle heroin into other countries. Often, bags of heroin are hidden inside the tyres and petrol tanks of vehicles and driven across borders. Sometimes the drug is concealed inside objects being transported, such as statues or furniture. But one of the most distressing methods of smuggling is the use of human **couriers**. These people – sometimes known as **mules** – swallow bags of heroin before they enter a country, and then wait for the bags to pass out through their digestive systems. Sometimes this has tragic results when a bag bursts or gets stuck.

The chain of dealers

Once supplies of heroin have been smuggled into a country, they are sold on to dealers. Dealing operates on many levels, with everyone taking some of the profits. However, while the dealers at the top of the chain earn huge profits, the dealers

Young heroin mule

Recently there have been several cases of children and teenagers being used as heroin mules. In April 2002, a twelve-year-old Nigerian-American agreed to become a mule because he was so desperate to return to his mother in the United States.

Soon after arriving in New York from Lagos, Prince Nnaedozie Umegbolu developed severe stomach pains. He was taken to hospital, where it was discovered that he had swallowed 87 condoms full of heroin. Doctors, who removed most of the condoms, said he could have died if any of them had burst. The boy said he had been offered US$1,900 (£1,000) to carry the drug to the United States.

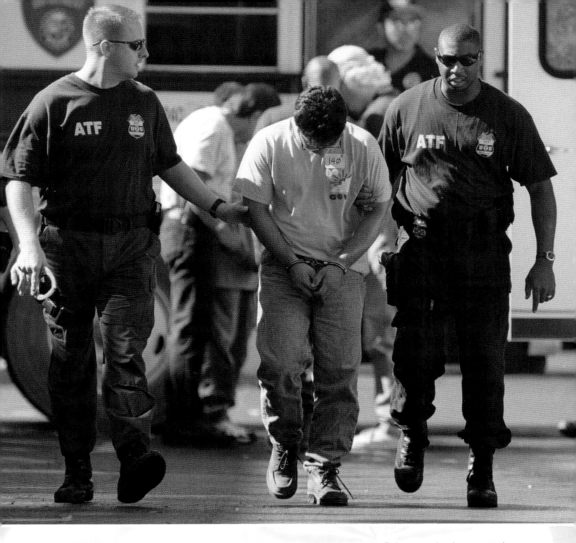

at the bottom of the chain, who are selling the drugs on the street, get much smaller profits. These people are almost always **addicts** themselves, so they are desperate for money, or simply need ready supplies of their drug.

Young people at risk

Today, it's not unusual for young people to be approached by dealers on the streets. The best thing to do in a situation like this is simply but firmly to say no. If a dealer sees that you are not interested they will usually stop bothering you. For more advice on strategies for saying no, see page 51.

❚ A smuggler is arrested by special drugs police in Florida, United States. People caught carrying drugs face long periods in jail. Meanwhile, the criminals who mastermind the operation usually manage to escape the law completely.

Heroin causes many problems for our society and especially for the people who have to deal with the damage. Doctors, social workers, and other health professionals all work hard to help the **addicts** and their families. Meanwhile, the police have the difficult job of dealing with the crime and violence caused by the illegal drugs business.

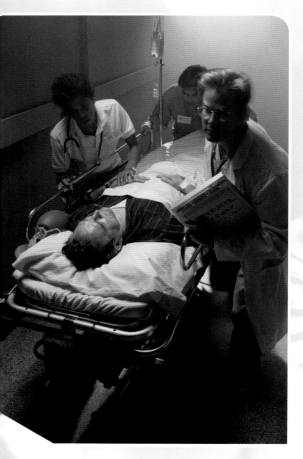

I Medical staff are faced with countless emergencies caused by heroin. Meanwhile, other patients may go untreated.

Medical care

Every year, many health professionals have to deal with thousands of emergencies related to heroin **abuse**. Addicts who have taken **overdoses**, or injected themselves with impure heroin, need immediate expert care. There is also the daily business of caring for people with illnesses caused by heroin use.

Helping addicts and their families

Heroin addicts need help in other ways too. If they have decided to try to kick their habit, they need the support of expert staff, either in hospitals or clinics. Addicts and their families may also need **psychological** help and **counselling** to help them deal with the problems in their lives.

Keeping people safe

People who take heroin do many things that put themselves and others at risk. Heroin addicts may break into shops, homes, and offices to steal money and property. They may get involved in violent fights – especially with drug **dealers**. Because many heroin addicts don't pay enough attention to safety, there are often fires and accidents in the places where they live. Addicts also tend to leave their needles lying around in public places. All of these problems pose a huge challenge for the police and the fire service, as they try to make life safer both for the heroin addicts and for the people around them.

> *"I can't tell you how many kids I've seen killed by heroin. And it's all down to those criminals who put the drugs on the streets."*
>
> Mike, a member of an Australian ambulance team

Keeping control

As well as working to keep the streets safe, the police have the very difficult job of trying to stop the spread of heroin use. The police are up against a network of dealers and smugglers, but they are also on the lookout for people who use heroin. In most countries of the world, heroin use is against the law, so part of the police's job is to discover the heroin users and arrest them, so that they can be prosecuted in court.

▌Children playing in parks run the risk of coming across discarded heroin needles. Abandoned needles may cause injury and spread infections such as **HIV**.

Governments today face many problems caused by heroin. First, there is the urgent need to stop the production of heroin and its illegal entry into countries worldwide. Then there is the vast network of **dealers** to be uncovered. What are governments doing to tackle these problems?

Beating the barons

Standing up to the power of the **drug barons** is a daunting task – and one that needs to be tackled internationally. The **United Nations (UN)** has tried to take the lead, surveying the situation worldwide and producing reports on what needs to be done. However, countries find it hard to cooperate in the fight against heroin. In many of the heroin-producing regions, governments are too poor to spend money fighting the barons. Many of these governments also gain part of their income from heroin.

❚ These police officers are using sniffer dogs, which are specially trained to track down drugs.

Major drugs haul

The struggle against drug smugglers and dealers uses up enormous amounts of money, time, and effort. But when the drug enforcement agencies succeed, they can make a real difference to a community. In November 2003, police arrested ten people and seized a large amount of heroin in a major drugs haul. The arrests were the result of an eighteen-month investigation into the Vista Homeboys. This gang was responsible for much of the violence and the flourishing heroin trade in the Vista community 40 miles north of San Diego, California.

"The shackles of drug intimidation have been removed from the community," said Michael S. Vigil, special agent in charge of the San Diego drug enforcement team. "When citizens call you in tears thanking you for getting rid of this cancerous cell from your community, I think that really highlights the negative impact they had."

Stopping the smuggling?
In recent years, many countries have introduced very tight border controls in an attempt to crack down on drug smuggling. Specially trained staff use scanning machines and sniffer dogs to help them root out hidden heroin stashes. However, this makes the smugglers even more determined, as they turn to dangerous practices, such as using human drug **couriers**.

Dealing with the dealers
It is an incredibly difficult task to detect all the secret drug deals that take place in homes, pubs, and clubs, and on the streets. However, special drug squads are trained to track down dealers, and when they uncover them the penalties are extremely severe. Heroin dealers can be given unlimited fines and very long jail sentences, with many of them facing life imprisonment.

What about the addicts?

Apart from coping with heroin smuggling and **dealing**, governments also face the pressing question of what to do about the heroin **addicts**. Heroin use causes many problems for society. How should governments approach this difficult problem?

Tough laws

In most countries the law on heroin use is very clear. In the United Kingdom, heroin is classified as a "Class A" drug and in the United States it is a "Schedule 1" drug. This means that it is recognized as one of the most dangerous drugs that can be used. It is against the law both to use heroin and to have it in your possession. **Possession** usually leads to a prison sentence of around five years and a heavy fine. **Supplying** heroin to others can lead to very long sentences – and even life imprisonment – and an unlimited fine. These tough laws send out a very clear message that taking heroin is a crime.

The prison problem

One consequence of the heavy jail sentences for heroin users is that a great strain is placed on the prison system. This is a particular problem in the United States, where there is serious overcrowding in prisons. Many addicts manage to obtain supplies of heroin while they are in jail. Meanwhile, by mixing with hardened criminals, addicts learn more about how to survive by crime. Studies show that after their release from prison, over half of the drug addicts will commit crimes and end up back in jail.

Seeking a solution

In order to find some workable solutions to the problems of heroin addiction, a range of schemes have been tried. In some "arrest referral" schemes, heroin addicts who are arrested for possession are sent immediately for addiction treatment. Some courts operate a credit system, whereby people found guilty of drug possession may be given lighter jail sentences if they agree to enter a treatment programme.

Heroin on prescription?

In the Netherlands, the Dutch government has tried a different approach to tackling the problem of heroin addiction. Here, small numbers of heroin addicts are issued with **prescriptions** for heroin. These registered addicts inject their drug in medically supervised injection rooms. This ensures that registered users get a safe supply of their drug, instead of buying impure heroin from dealers.

It is too early to judge whether the Dutch approach is making any significant difference, but the Dutch government hopes that it will help to reduce the power of the heroin dealers. Switzerland has introduced a similar scheme. However, other governments think that the Dutch scheme sends out a dangerous message to addicts that taking heroin is not a crime.

❚ Our prisons today face serious problems of overcrowding. Is prison really the answer for heroin addicts?

Are there things that worry you about heroin? If there are –
either now or in the future – there are lots of people and
places you can contact. Many organizations offer help
and advice on problems related to heroin. You can call
a telephone helpline at any time, and there are trained
counsellors to talk through problems and help find solutions.

*"What I say to anyone who's
tempted to try heroin is
just look at me. I wasted
seventeen years of my life –
years I'll never get back. I
nearly died lots of times and
I lost some of my closest
friends. Heroin has no
mercy – all you can do is
keep away from it."*

Ben, an ex-heroin addict

Finding out more

If you want to find out more about
heroin and the issues associated
with it, you can start by contacting
the organizations listed at the
back of this book. Many of them
have useful websites and some
supply information packs.

Someone to talk to

Sometimes it can be hard to talk
to people you know about the
things that are worrying you. You
may want to discuss your concerns
in confidence, knowing that
whatever you say won't be passed
on to anyone you know.

▌ If you make the wrong decision about drugs, the future could end up looking pretty grim.

Fortunately, there's an easy way to find somebody sympathetic to talk to. Many organizations have telephone helplines, and their phones are staffed by specially trained advisers. You don't have to have a heroin problem yourself to call. You will find details of drugs organizations and telephone helplines on pages 54–55 of this book.

It's up to you

Are you worried that sometime in the future you might be offered heroin? You may be sure that you don't want to try it, but explaining that to a persuasive friend or **dealer** may be hard. It's important to remember that, whatever people say, it's OK to say no to drugs. Here are some things you can do to put yourself less at risk:

- Be prepared. Think over what you'll say in advance if you are offered heroin.

- Never forget the dangers. Taking heroin – even just once – can ruin your life.

- Remember you're not alone. There are telephone numbers to call and people you can talk to about your worries.

- Most of all remember – it's your life. Nobody else can tell you what to do. It's up to you to make your own decisions.

▌ It's up to you to choose whether you want to enjoy your life and make the most of your opportunities.

Glossary

abuse use of drugs for non-medical reasons in a way that has a bad effect

addiction when a person is unable to manage without a drug, and finds it extremely hard to stop using it

anaemia medical condition caused by not having enough healthy red cells in the blood. People with anaemia feel tired all the time.

antidote drug that cancels out the effect of another drug

central nervous system network of nerves that runs from the brain through the spine and controls all the movements of the body

chase/chase the dragon sniff up the fumes from a line of burning heroin powder

circulation movement of blood around the body

clean not taking drugs

codeine painkilling drug that can be bought in tablets from a pharmacy

cold turkey when a person suddenly stops taking drugs

counselling advice and guidance given to help people resolve their problems

courier someone who carries drugs across a border for somebody else

crave feel a strong or uncontrollable need or longing for something

cut mix with another substance

dealer someone who buys and sells illegal drugs

dependence when a person is unable to cope without a drug

detoxification (detox) when all traces of a drug are gradually removed from a person's body

developed country rich industrialized country

diamorphine medical name for heroin

drug baron someone who controls the supplies of a drug

epidemic widespread occurrence of an infectious disease

fix dose of a drug to which one is addicted

hepatitis infection caused by a virus, which can seriously damage the liver

HIV virus that can lead to AIDS

hooked addicted

in confidence privately, without telling anyone else

inhale take smoke into the lungs

intravenous injected into a vein

junkie someone who is addicted to a drug

malnutrition condition in which someone does not have enough nourishment (good, healthy food) in their body

media TV, cinema, magazines, and newspapers, and any other forms of mass communication

methadone medical drug that has some similar effects to heroin, but does not make people "high"

miscarriage loss of a baby because it has died inside the womb, usually early in pregnancy

morphine painkilling drug derived from opium, used medically to relieve pain

mule someone who carries illegal drugs over a border. Mules sometimes swallow bags containing drugs.

nausea feeling of wanting to vomit

opiate any substance made from the fluid found in the opium poppy. Opiates have the effect of reducing awareness of pain.

opium drug produced from the opium poppy, which can be smoked

opium den place where people go to smoke opium. Opium dens were common in China in the eighteenth and nineteenth centuries.

overdose excessive dose of a drug, which the body cannot cope with

pneumonia inflammation of the lungs

possession owning or having an illegal drug (either carrying it or having it hidden somewhere)

prescribe to write an instruction (a prescription) that authorizes a medicine to be given to a patient

prescription instruction written by a doctor that authorizes a medicine to be given to a patient

prostitution receiving money in return for having sex

psychological to do with or affecting the mind, emotions, and behaviour

receptor area of the brain that responds to a drug in a certain way

snort take a drug by sniffing it up the nose

sterile totally clean and free from bacteria

substitution when one substance or drug is replaced by a different one

supply give or sell drugs to other people

terrorist someone who uses violence to try to change things in the world

therapy treatment that helps someone to get better. Therapy often involves talking.

tolerance need for larger and larger doses of a drug to get the same effect

tuberculosis serious lung disease in which the lungs are gradually destroyed. Tuberculosis can often result in death.

United Nations (UN) international organization that was set up to deal with world problems

virus organism that multiplies inside the body, causing disease

withdrawal symptoms unpleasant physical and mental feelings experienced during the process of giving up an addictive drug

There are a number of organizations that provide information and advice about drugs. Some have helpful websites, or provide information packs and leaflets, while others offer help and support over the phone.

Contacts in the United Kingdom

Adfam
Waterbridge House, 32–36 Loman Street, London SE1 0EH
Tel: 020 7928 8898
www.adfam.org.uk
Adfam is a national charity that gives confidential support and information to families and friends of drug users. They also run family-support groups.

Childline
Tel: 0800 1111
A 24-hour number for any young person in distress to call. It offers confidential help and guidance from trained counsellors on a range of issues, including family problems caused by heroin.

Connexions Direct
Helpline: 080 800 13219
(8 a.m.–2 a.m. daily)
Text: 07766 4 13219
www.connexions-direct.com
This service for young people aged from thirteen to nineteen offers information and advice on a wide range of topics, including drugs. Young people can also speak to an adviser by telephone, webchat, email, or text message.

DrugScope
32–36 Loman Street, London SE1 0EE
Tel: 020 7928 1211
www.drugscope.org.uk
A national drugs information agency with services that include a library, a wide range of publications, and a website.

Families Anonymous
Doddington & Rollo Community Association, Charlotte Despard Avenue, Battersea, London SW11 5HD
Helpline: 0845 1200 660
www.famanon.org.uk
An organization involved in support groups for parents and families of drug users. They can put you in touch with groups in different parts of the country.

FRANK
Tel: 0800 776600
Email: frank@talktofrank.com
www.talktofrank.com
An organization for young people that gives free, confidential advice and information about drugs 24 hours a day.

Narcotics Anonymous
UK Service Office, 202 City Road, London EC1V 2PH
Helpline: 020 7730 0009
(10 a.m.–10 p.m. daily)
www.ukna.org
A fellowship of people who have given up narcotics, using a twelve-step programme. They have a helpline for users and their friends and relatives, plus events and meetings around the United Kingdom.

Release
Helpline: 0845 4500 215
(10 a.m.–5.30 p.m. Mon–Fri)
Email: ask@release.org.uk
www.release.org.uk
An organization that provides legal advice to drug users, their families, and friends. The advice is free, professional, and confidential.